MW01518530

Facts About the Snowy Owl

By Lisa Strattin

© 2022 Lisa Strattin

FREE BOOK

FREE FOR ALL SUBSCRIBERS

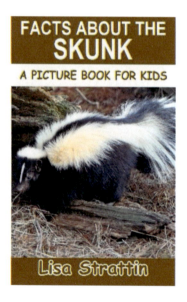

LisaStrattin.com/Subscribe-Here

BOX SET

- **FACTS ABOUT THE POISON DART FROGS**
- **FACTS ABOUT THE THREE TOED SLOTH**
- **FACTS ABOUT THE RED PANDA**
- **FACTS ABOUT THE SEAHORSE**
- **FACTS ABOUT THE PLATYPUS**
- **FACTS ABOUT THE REINDEER**
- **FACTS ABOUT THE PANTHER**
- **FACTS ABOUT THE SIBERIAN HUSKY**

LisaStrattin.com/BookBundle

Facts for Kids Picture Books by Lisa Strattin

Little Blue Penguin, Vol 92

Chipmunk, Vol 5

Frilled Lizard, Vol 39

Blue and Gold Macaw, Vol 13

Poison Dart Frogs, Vol 50

Blue Tarantula, Vol 115

African Elephants, Vol 8

Amur Leopard, Vol 89

Sabre Tooth Tiger, Vol 167

Baboon, Vol 174

Sign Up for New Release Emails Here

LisaStrattin.com/subscribe-here

All rights reserved. No part of this book may be reproduced by any means whatsoever without the written permission from the author, except brief portions quoted for purpose of review.

All information in this book has been carefully researched and checked for factual accuracy. However, the author and publisher makes no warranty, express or implied, that the information contained herein is appropriate for every individual, situation or purpose and assume no responsibility for errors or omissions. The reader assumes the risk and full responsibility for all actions, and the author will not be held responsible for any loss or damage, whether consequential, incidental, special or otherwise, that may result from the information presented in this book.

All images are free for use or purchased from stock photo sites or royalty free for commercial use.

Some coloring pages might be of the general species due to lack of available images.

I have relied on my own observations as well as many different sources for this book and I have done my best to check facts and give credit where it is due. In the event that any material is used without proper permission, please contact me so that the oversight can be corrected.

★★COVER IMAGE★★

https://www.flickr.com/photos/wildreturn/8287891515/

★★ADDITIONAL IMAGES★★

https://www.flickr.com/photos/jonnyb558/8681081380/

https://www.flickr.com/photos/hisgett/4335228182/

https://www.flickr.com/photos/loshak/5161217389/

https://www.flickr.com/photos/53344659@N05/4979048548/

https://www.flickr.com/photos/132033298@N04/24937699785/

https://www.flickr.com/photos/harlequeen/2975128222/

https://www.flickr.com/photos/winnu/6777063045/

https://www.flickr.com/photos/15016964@N02/8492250841/

https://www.flickr.com/photos/68069539@N07/41561591952/

https://www.flickr.com/photos/wwarby/4916260752/

Contents

INTRODUCTION

The Snowy Owl is a large, white owl of the true owl family. They are native to the Arctic regions and tundra in North America and Eurasia. However, they have also been spotted in other cold areas like Alaska, Canada, Europe, and Russia. Some nicknames for the Snowy Owl include *Arctic Owl*, *Great White Owl*, *Ghost Owl*, *Tundra Ghost*, and *White Terror of the North*. It is the official bird of Quebec.

The scientific name of the Snowy Owl is *Bubo Scandiacus*.

CHARACTERISTICS

They are usually solitary birds, only coming together for the breeding season. During the breeding season, these owls collect and store food around the nest. They do this to create a stockpile so that they can have food even when hunting prey is scarce when the owlets are born.

They communicate mainly through hoots, mews, hisses, and 'kre-kre' sounds, to defend their nest or hunting ground from others. They are also migratory birds, meaning that they can cover vast areas and fly to other places to hunt for more food. However, their migratory timing is sporadic, and there is no true sense of when these birds migrate, only that they do.

Although they are also diurnal, thanks to the Arctic sun and reflections from the snow, they hunt and are most active during the day and sleep at night, which is the opposite of most other owl species.

APPEARANCE

Males are almost all white, while females have more flecks of black plumage. The females are bigger than the males, and their thick feathers make them 4 pounds heavier. Juvenile Snowy Owls are heavily barred. Some birds may retain some of their juvenile plumage throughout their first winter.

A Snowy Owl's bill is black, and the cere (flesh around the base of the bill) is yellow. The legs and feet are covered in thick feathers, which help keep the owl warm in its Arctic habitat. Their feet also have extra padding, so the cold doesn't bother them when they are on or in the snow. They have fantastic eyesight but also a powerful sense of smell. They can sense if their prey is under the snow and can dive down to the correct place to capture their prey.

LIFE STAGES

There are four main life stages for the Snowy Owl. They start from an egg to a hatchling, the juvenile stage, and finally, a fully formed adult.

A female Snowy Owl will lay between 1 and 11 eggs in a *clutch*. The eggs are white and elliptical. They are incubated for right around one month. The Snowy Owl chicks are covered in downy feathers when the eggs hatch. They are not yet able to fly, but they can climb and perch. They are dependent on their parents for food and shelter at this stage.

Juvenile Snowy Owls start to grow their adult feathers at around three months old. Finally, they gain their full adult plumage at around nine months old. They are fully independent and can mate and start their own families at this stage.

Snowy Owls are also monogamous during the breeding time, meaning that the pair will stay together during that breeding season and then find a new partner for the next.

LIFE SPAN

The Snowy Owl typically lives for around ten years in the wild and 20 years in captivity. However, there have been reports of Snowy Owls living for over 30 years in captivity!

SIZE

The Snowy Owl is a large bird, with a typical length of 20 to 27 inches and a wingspan of 53 to 60 inches. It also has one of the heaviest bodies for the size of any North American owl, typically weighing 2.6 to 4.5 pounds.

Snowy Owls are among the fastest flying owls, with speeds reaching up to 60 miles per hour.

HABITAT

Snowy Owls build their nests on the ground, using whatever materials they can gather, such as rocks, bones, feathers, and rubbish. They often return to the same nest site year after year. Their natural habitat is cold, without trees, and adapted to this environment.

DIET

The Snowy Owl is a carnivore and primarily preys on lemmings and voles, although it will also eat other small rodents, birds, reptiles, and insects. Occasionally, Snowy Owls have been known to kill rabbits, weasels, and foxes. The Snowy Owl hunts primarily during the day but will also hunt at night if necessary. When prey is scarce, Snowy Owls have been known to scavenge on carcasses left by other animals.

The Snowy Owl typically hunts by perching on a high vantage point, waiting for prey to come within range. Once prey is spotted, the Snowy Owl swoops down and snatches it up with its talons. The Snowy Owl will then fly back to its perch and eat prey.

ENEMIES

The Snowy Owl only has a few natural predators. Foxes and wolves will hunt them when the owls are near their nests.

SUITABILITY AS PETS

While Snowy Owls are undeniably beautiful creatures, they are not well-suited to be kept as pets. Snowy Owls are wild animals, and their instincts can pose a danger to themselves and their would-be owners. In addition, they require a particular diet and environment difficult for most people to provide.

There are many other birds that are more suitable for you to keep as a pet. You can visit your local pet store and ask questions about birds as pets from a staff member there.

COLOR ME

COLOR ME

COLOR ME

COLOR ME

COLOR ME

COLOR ME

COLOR ME

COLOR ME

COLOR ME

COLOR ME